T0064013

WHO KILLED CUSTOMER CARE?

KEN WELSH

PARTRIDGE
A Penguin Random House Company

www.letstalkcommunication.com
www.kenwelsh.biz
www.kenwelsh.com
ken@kenwelsh.com

Illustrations by Jonathan Han

To order additional copies of this book, contact
Toll Free 800 101 2657 (Singapore)
Toll Free 1 800 81 7340 (Malaysia)
orders.singapore@partridgepublishing.com

www.partridgepublishing.com/singapore

I dedicate this book my fantastic father and best mate,
Don Welsh.

CONTENTS

ACKNOWLEDGMENTS

This book could never have been written without the trust, support, and relentless faith of my champion Mike Faith (excuse the pun) and his amazing team at Headsets.com (San Francisco and Nashville). Also of invaluable importance in formulating this book were my wonderful friends at Wayside Technology (New Jersey), Los Ninos (New York), Plamex (Mexico), Class Act (South Africa), and Leichardt Council (Australia).

They helped me learn as I coached them, and they gave me great joy and friendship through it all.

And of course thank you to my amazing partner, Francesca Cordeaux, and my mother, Marcia Welsh, for their tireless support and encouragement.

And here's to the incredible Customer Care standards set by organizations around the world that strive for ever-improving levels of service excellence.

Things happen!

Anything that happens, happens for a reason.

Anything that doesn't happen for a reason, doesn't happen.

Anything that, in happening, creates a reason for anything else to happen, has, itself, a reason for happening.

Anything that, in happening, may cause itself to happen again, is likely to happen again . . . and again . . . and again . . . and again . . .

However, we can help it happen better—every time!

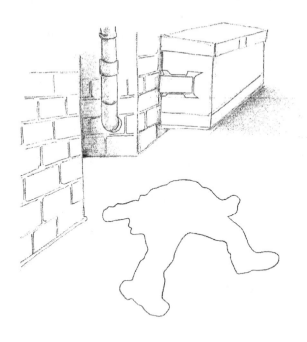

CHAPTER 1

THE END ... WELL, ALMOST!

Three things happened simultaneously in a world where, usually, millions of things happen—just because they do.

Or do they?

As news banners flashed across the screen, network anchors spread the word with the artificial sadness of a reporter torn between the need to appear to care and the euphoria of a breaking-news tragedy—Redman Folgate was dead!

"The billionaire entrepreneur's body has been found in his secret mountain retreat known as "Folgate's Secret Mountain Retreat". The man who expanded Customer Service to include

'Internal Customers,' 'Interpersonal Customers,' and even 'the Customer in You'—a Customer himself and known to the world as "Mr Customer Care"—is dead at forty-seven years of age, his retail empire in tatters."

*   *   *

Julia, Folgate's devastatingly gorgeous, much younger wife, sat quietly sobbing on their double king-sized bed in their Belle Vue Hacienda.

"How could it have come to this?"

*   *   *

Through unseasonable, if not unheard-of, torrential rain, subdued light flickered in the window of a small, spartan room attached to the Lamb's Bar, Lower Mullumdabba, in the outback of Australia.

Rock Hardstuff, rural reporter for the *City & Country E-Journal*, watched text projected onto the gray wall from his wrist communicator. The information was sporadic; out here wireless text reception was still unreliable. The words flashed on the wall:

"Your story dumped . . . revolutionary sheep breeding . . . old hat . . . No Play No Pay."

Funny how they managed to get that last piece of information through in full.

Rock hit the "Headline" button.

"Market Crashes . . . Empire Collapses . . . Who . . . the . . . F . . . Cares"

The messages struck a chord with Hardstuff.

Moral: There is always someone who cares.

CHAPTER 2

IN THE BEGINNING

Rain had always been a welcome sight in the outback, but today Mullumdabba's townsfolk had turned out to say farewell to their favorite son. And a wet funeral seemed so inappropriate for this boy from the bush. Today tears and beers should have been the only liquids.

Local minister Howard Rightly summed up Walter Folgate as "a force to be reckoned with . . . a man of old-fashioned values, perhaps, though clearly one who knew what he wanted and what other people wanted."

Walter's department store, simply called The Store, had been the heart, if not the soul, of Mullumdabba for some thirty years, and now Folgate's only son, Redman Folgate, would take the reins.

All six of The Store's staff stood in silence as one thought simultaneously occupied their minds: "What will happen next?" Red was so young, and his only real interests were breeding his award-winning pet sheep—Spanish Merinos crossed with black-faced Mexican Tzotzil sheep. Ten gold medals in ten years! And, of course, his general love of all things Mexican.

All Red had ever done in The Store was help them pack shelves. And now their future rested, unstably, in his childlike hands: Would he sell The Store to those big-city folks who had been pestering Walter for so long?

The following days did little to assuage their fears.

Red spent much of his time caring for his mother or playing sports with former school friends. He had little regard for The Store, assuming that it could run itself.

The funny thing was—it more or less did.

Moral: Some things are good the way they are; always remember, however, *that "good" is often used as an excuse for not quite being "great" or—even worse—for merely being "satisfactory"!*

CHAPTER 3

MESSAGE RECEIVED

In a fitful sleep, Rock dreamed of jungle, war, and hovercopters. Rain beat down, and the whoosh of a single rescue hovercopter shook the lianas and covered him with spray from the nearby jungle giants—banyans lassoed in a tangle of vines. As he lay there wounded and crippled with pain, trapped and unable to call for the rescue team for fear that the enemy would find him first, drops of water from the trees above punched his battered face.

Rock's mind rebelled against the dream. "You have never been in the jungle, let alone a war."

As he drifted back to the dream, the water was now dripping off the back of a black-faced sheep. The sheep ducked for cover as bullets sprayed the jungle, and water cascaded from its back across Rock's face.

Again his mind rebelled. "The last good war was when I was twelve, and all I could do was dream of reporting it!"

Dream—damn! It's a bloody dream again. Rock jarred himself into the conscious world.

The leak from the ceiling had moved as the rain intensified and was now aimed squarely at his forehead.

There he sat, saturated in reality—the reality of a rural reporter stuck in the last hick town for the last sheep sale of the year. The most exciting news to date had been the development of a new sheep dip that could be used on spring lambs and would protect them for the rest of their lives. It did make the meat toxic, but the wool was okay. And this was a wool town!

Why bother sleeping? He could do that at the sale. He'd just check the wireless text news for prices and write his article based on that.

Speaking of which—would it be working now? He proudly fired up his new TeleTexta WC350N wrist communicator again.

Text came and went on the gray wall. The reception was gradually improving as Rock twisted a metal coat hanger that ran from his hand, the current home of his WC350N, to the curtain rod.

One final chance, one final stretch—Rock tugged at the curtain rod in a last-ditch effort. The rod crashed to the floor, then bounced into the sink, finally coming to rest on the rusted metal of the cold-water faucet—and the wall came to life. Text and images barraged the senses as Rock's WC350N made up for lost time by deluging him with pent-up information.

First the network logo—"The Sea of *Cs*," they called it—a series of animated waves breaking across the screen, forming rows of the letter *C* moments before they broke and dissolved into foam. Instantly the foam built itself into images of skyscrapers and then farms and houses and then back to nothingness. "You have sixty-two new messages" flashed from his wrist.

Message Subjects:

TeleTexta apologizes for any inconvenience that you may be experiencing. Severe flooding in your area has restricted access for service crews. Until such time as regular service can be renewed, twice daily downloads will be initiated.

Estimated rectification of your fault is anticipated to be indeterminable due to severe flooding. Severe flooding in your area has restricted access for service crews to permit them to determine the estimated time to repair your fault. At this time no service crews are currently available to determine how long it will take the other service crews to determine how long it will take your service crew to rectify your fault.

TeleTexta hopes that this satisfies your inquiry. To submit a Customer Satisfaction Survey form and to place yourself in the running to win a new, state-of-the-art TeleTexta Wrist Communicator WC400S, please press the red button on your outmoded WC350N. Otherwise please feel free to press the green button to return to your message summaries.

TeleTexta wishes you a happy, profitable, and communicative day.

Rock pressed green. He couldn't afford to press red.

> Message 1: Folgate Dead . . .
> Message 2: Folgate Dead . . .
> Message 3: Folgate Dead . . .
> Message 4: Folgate Dead . . .
> Message 5: Folgate Dead . . .
> Message 6: Folgate Dead . . .
> Message 7: Folgate Dead . . .
> Message 8: Folgate Dead . . .
> There was a brief pause.
> Then . . .
> Message 9: Folgate Dead . . .

Rock hit the Headline button.

> Stock Market Crashes. International Retail Empire Collapses due to Founder's Death. Who Was the Real Redman Folgate? Founder of "The Store That Cares."

Rock hit the Details button.

> Redman Folgate died alone in his secret mountain retreat located at 465 Snowy Peak Road, Mount Beauty. Share prices around the world tumble as rumors of Folgate's suicide spread.
>
> The sleepy town of Mullumdabba braces for paparazzi as Folgate's body is returned home for the funeral.

The text field faded and then briefly spluttered back to life.

Thank you for using TeleTexta E-Communication, a division of City & Country E-Nterprises, satisfying customers for a century.

Mullumdabba. The name lingered on the wall and then faded as Rock mused: "Mullumdabba. That name rings a bell."

The name blinked once more and then disappeared—another blackout!

*   *   *

Hotel guests struggled in the darkness, the lucky ones with matches, the very lucky ones without. As Rock made his way down the hall, the grotesque, flocked wallpaper took on a life of its own, mocking him with images of wealth and opulence.

In reality they were merely velvet stripes decorated with innumerable stains from overexuberantly opened beer-can sprays.

As Rock approached the reception desk, knowing full well that he would be complaining to deaf ears about the fifth blackout in three days, he heard music—loud music—and laughter in the bar.

The town had packed into The Lamb's Bar, and a wake was in full swing.

"Turn the bloody music down, Cheryl!" a short, gray-haired man yelled to the receptionist. "What are you, bloody deaf?"

"Yes," the aging receptionist replied in sign language punctuated by a gesture readily translated into any language.

Power or no power, the passing of the town's dear son would not go unnoticed. The hotel's generator had all its power diverted to the bar.

With a glass thrust into his hand and the demand "Drink up, stranger" shouted at him, Rock obliged.

He soon found himself singing along with the townsfolk in their tribute to someone called Red, "Our boy, Red."

Soon a new game erupted as alcoholically lubricated locals matched wits in what appeared to be a poem of sorts. Or perhaps it was more a ritual chant:

"Mull. Mullum. Mullumdabba. Mullumdabba . . . dabba . . . doooooo!"

Cheers and laughter erupted.

Mullumdabba . . . Folgate . . . Red!

*   *   *

He was a successful man—a *very* successful man—and successful men have enemies! Did he just die or was he killed? Was it possible that fate, for once in Rock's unremarkable life, had remarkably placed him in exactly the right place at exactly the right time? While everyone else would be investigating crime scenes, digging through forensic reports, and looking at autopsy tapes, Rock would be the one reporter locked away with a town full of Folgate's friends, isolated until the floodwaters abated.

This was, without a doubt, Rock's one chance at a ticket out of rural reporting!

Breaking news, here I come, he thought.

A dash to his room, a crash in the dark, and then back to the bar he was, with his Digi Dicta in hand. The pickle-sized digital recorder would catch every word, every piece of gossip that the lubricated locals would throw his way. What was the real goss on Redman Folgate? What was he really like? "Tyrant, Terror, or Titmouse?"

"Titmouse"? He'd have to come up with a better title later. For now, he'd get the story down.

Rock loomed at the door, ready to pounce.

First victim—the old, gray-haired lady near the fireplace; the old, gray-haired man near the window; the old, gray . . . was that a man or a woman near the cellar door?

It suddenly struck him: they were all old and gray.

What was it with this town? They certainly had enough blackouts to be surrounded by children—, but there was no one under sixty, maybe—fifty, definitely.

He'd never noticed it before. Then again, he'd spent most of his time at the sale yards reporting on the prices of woolly wethers and two-year-old rams.

Moral: Sometimes the obvious isn't so obvious, especially if you're sitting right in the middle of it.

CHAPTER 4

THE LAMB'S BAR

"There, yes, over there. A tall, slim, gorgeous—my God, she is gorgeous! Young, slim, firm, redhead—absolutely delicious."

Rock blinked himself back to reality. "I've got to get out of rural reporting,"—it's a sheep—Dolly, the bar's mascot.

"Nah, Dolly's a platinum blonde," spouted Neville. "She may be cute, and, although she was Redman's favorite, I wouldn't say she was gorgeous."

Neville was right. Dolly was a platinum blonde, and Rock's eyes had caught a fleeting glimpse of flame in the mirror behind the bar.

Absolutely. A fiery redhead, much younger than the throng of gray-haired locals. Who was she?

And, more important, where was she now?

As Rock wandered, he wondered if this simply was another bad dream brought on by long-term abuse of substances like coffee and chocolate. He knew that his parents had warned him in his early years, and he'd avoided temptation until his fifth girlfriend seduced him with a mocha megachino, and then, his ultimate downfall, too many springs ago even to think about—Venice, a balmy Sunday afternoon, and an *affogato* topped with chocolate sprinkles! Indeed, that was many, many, years ago, in a completely different life.

As a competent reporter, he knew of all the studies that had sung the praises of the brown brew's chlorogenic acids, melanoids, antioxidants, and caffeine. They postponed Parkinson's, deferred diabetes, cleaned the colon, canceled the chances of cirrhosis, and aided attentiveness. Not to mention the benefits of chocolate—he knew better than to mention the benefits of chocolate!

As Rock wandered, he also pondered. Weren't there studies in the last century that had also sung the praises of the now-outlawed pastime, tobacco smoking? Studies produced by notable medical researchers employed by equally notable companies that manufactured cigarettes. Surely it was purely coincidental that the coffee studies were funded by companies like Bean Busy, Ground Zero, and Mocha Do about Muffins.

Enough of that. *Back to the bad dream*, he thought.

Here he was, standing in The Lamb's Bar in Mullumdabba, surrounded by gray-haired, old people, searching for a redhead. It shouldn't be too hard, given the ambient grayness surrounding him. A solitary redhead—not much to ask for. Okay, one young, tall, firm, gorgeous, alluring, tantalizing, intelligent—how could he say *intelligent* when he'd never spoken with her?

"Nothing wrong with wishful thinking," chimed in Neville, setting Rock back several paces in thought. Or so he thought.

"No, you're pretty much where you were—Lamb's Bar, sea of gray heads, searching for a redhead."

"Neville, isn't it?"

"Absolutely. Neville Roman, spelled R-O-J-O-M-A-N, pronounced Roman. Neville will do."

"My head . . . you . . . out of it . . . now!"

"Anything you say."

"Or think," added Rock.

"I was sure you'd like to meet Julia. You're doing a story on Redman Folgate, aren't you?"

Moral: Choreograph your conversation like a motion picture. Start on a high and finish on a high. Then, even if you sink to the depths in the middle, your message will be received and remembered and will be more likely to be acted on.

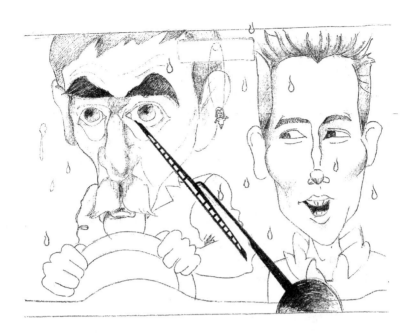

CHAPTER 5

ONCE AGAIN . . . BEFORE

U nheard-of-three weeks of continuous drizzle!
Since Walter's death, life in the small town had been cold and wet.

Nothing was dry anymore—rugs, sheets, walls, and clothes. Especially the clothes—his clothes. There was nothing that Red liked less than cold, wet socks. Well, maybe one or two other things. However, at the moment they weren't at the forefront of his mind. He wanted to be warm and dry.

The Store had air-conditioning. Maybe it was worth checking in.

* * *

One last effort, one last stretch. The final turn of the key, and Red would forget about The Store if the old Toyota didn't start.

All was silent but for an *aargh* as Red's knuckles jammed against the dashboard. He exited the car with his usual brash disdain, and the slammed door brought a cascade of cold droplets down his back as the adjacent wattle tree shook itself dry. Talk about cold! Talk about wet!

A warm hand on Red's shoulder took the chill from his veins with the offer of "A lift to The Store?" A solid man in his midforties had appeared from nowhere.

Dave Hazle was renowned as The Store's all-around-nice-guy, not just because he was nice in every way, but also in every place! Dave always seemed to know where to be, when to be there, and exactly what to do once he was there. He even had a reputation for ordering a Customer's items before the Customer knew that he or she needed them.

"So that they'd be ready for them when they realized," he'd say.

Red gladly climbed into Dave's old car.

Next thing they were in front of The Store, and Anne Harris was opening Red's door, umbrella in hand. As soon as she saw Red to the door, she was greeting Kerri Faithful in a similar manner.

Red blinked as various shop assistants dashed past with umbrellas, helping to ensure that the Customer Dampness Ratio was kept to a minimum.

As Red himself entered, a cup of warm cocoa was presented on a platter.

"Warm the cockles, young man!" Greeting him was Max Howard. Suddenly recognizing Red, Max hastened to add, "Sorry about the 'young man' bit."

"This must be costing us a fortune," said Red.

"Not as much as you'd think," added Dave as he downed his cocoa.

Red started to reply. No, he'd heard about Dave and wasn't going to humor his sort of behavior. His father had let it all go on for far too long. Still, he was great with the people, and he was retiring soon. *We do need another Dave.* Red's mind contorted as he looked at the staff. *Who could replace Dave? Would he really be such a loss?*

To cover for his open mouth, Red resolved to ask about the accounts.

Saying, "You'll be wanting to see the books," Dave opened the door to the office. It was his first time since Red's father's death. Memories of childhood play flooded through his mind—things like his methodical filing of a fish under *F* in his father's filing cabinet, only to be amazed at the reprimand that he had received two weeks later when the office was being fumigated and freshened. Mind you, his father had started the reprimand in such a way—"I see you've learned your alphabet well"—that the young Red wasn't sure whether he was to be disciplined or rewarded.

Walter always had a way of softening a blow with a positive message first, assuring that he got exactly what he wanted from people.

"About time someone has to see some sense in this place," grunted Bottomline Billy, Walter's bookkeeper, jarring Red from his thoughts. "A total rehash is what's in order."

He proudly plunked the paperwork in front of Red, as if to say, "I told him so!"

For days Red trudged through the books. After a while, he felt that he knew what was happening and then, suddenly, he didn't have any idea at all. Even knocking the phone off the hook to stop the interruptions didn't help. Probably because there hadn't been any interrupting phone calls to date.

Perhaps there was an answer—an obscure, tightly camouflaged, possibly even invisible answer. The trouble was that he had no idea whatsoever what the question was!

His efforts had held him at his father's—no, his—desk, for five days and four nights, toilet breaks and meals excluded. Dave pretty much anticipated his need for meals, which just seemed to arrive moments before Red realized that he was hungry.

Still, he had no idea where the profit was recorded—perhaps it was in a separate book.

"No separate book," Dave's voice echoed from the Customer Inquiry Counter, where he was happily telling Mrs. Welsh that he'd already ordered new trays for her Convection Plus oven—the ones that she'd be needing in two weeks' time.

Red knew that The Store had operated successfully for some thirty years. Now he realized that he'd only thought it had. All that the numbers indicated was that they'd paid employees, paid rent and utilities, and sold things to people. And year after year, the bottom line continued unperturbed—zero dollars.

Red pondered his predicament. "If this was the case, why hadn't Dad sold it to City & Country Discounters? They had been after it for at least five years."

Again Dave chimed in from his counter. "Because they put 'city' first, yet they treat their Customers like common sheep. That's what your dad always said. Besides, he never liked the attitude of their salespeople—city slickers in white slacks with Pure Newe Wool sport coats." Dave thought that this description pretty much summed up City & Country.

The Store had to make a profit. Was it really a case of Walter eating into the family savings to pay for food and his son's education?

The family had had vacations. Red knew that they'd had vacations—sometime, somewhere. He searched his memory. Yes, there'd been an aged aunt whom he'd lovingly called "My Dear Aged Aunt" for many years. There was a big house too. How old had he been—six or seven, maybe? Yes, he remembered her. It had been his eighth birthday, and she hadn't come to see him. She didn't come to see him ever again, and he didn't go away on vacation after that. He'd simply thought that was the way it was meant to be.

He might have been wrong, though. His mother always organized those sorts of things.

My God. My mother! he thought. *What happened to her?* He hadn't been home for five days!

Red's mind filled with images of his mother squeezing her last tea bag for its tenth cup and longingly looking at television commercials for cereal as she sucked on her one remaining stale rice flake, trying to resurrect its cardboard flavor for her final meal before she expired because of her inability to adjust the air-conditioning controls.

"Perhaps you'd best go home for a bit," Dave said quietly from the office door, car keys in hand.

This time Red took his advice without question.

Moral: If you start with a positive message, you're more likely to have your message well received.

Chapter 6

GONE, THOUGH NOT FORGOTTEN

The house was deathly quiet as Red wandered from room to room. Everything was in its place. Everything was where he had left it—except, of course, his mother.

Her bed was made. Her denture glass was clean. Her curtain was drawn against the devastatingly hot sun.

For the first time Red noticed that the rain had abated.

His mother's wardrobe was empty. Her room's air conditioner was set to "cool."

Wardrobe: empty. Place for clothes: should be full, now empty.

Red's mind grappled with this as he continued to check the other rooms.

No dirty plates. Table cleared except for a note. Plenty of food in the refrigerator—the milk was a little curdled, more like yogurt, though some people like yogurt, and it would be perfect for sourdough pancakes.

Wardrobe empty! Reality, at last, permeated his blinkered mind and suddenly hit him with the full force of an angry Customer returning her faulty sewing machine for the fourth time.

Someone had come in and robbed them. They'd stolen all his mother's clothes!

Red's mind filled with images of his mother, now naked, squeezing her last tea bag for its tenth cup and longingly looking at television commercials for cereal as she . . . No, the thought was too much for even Red to imagine.

He shook his head in disbelief. How could they?

As his head shook, he saw blurred images of the note on the kitchen table. "Why is it blurred?" he wondered out loud.

"Because you're shaking your head," Dave blurted out as he walked into the kitchen. "Stop shaking it."

In recognition of the magnitude and accuracy of Dave's advice to date, Red did as instructed.

Momentarily his eyes refocused. There was indeed a note.

Dear Red,

Tried to call you. The line was always busy. I do worry about you talking so much. It must be because you had so little to say as a child.

Anyway, have decided to go and see the world before it's too late.

Remember how I always wanted to see Paris and Venice and Egypt and New York and . . .

Well, I'll be in Las Vegas if you need me.
Look after The Store and have fun.

Your Mum

Moral: We like to think that our parents will always be there for us—they won't. Sometimes people need to be there just for themselves. Sometimes you need to be your own most important Customer.

Chapter 7

THE HERE AND THE NOW

"At least that's how I recall it. I took Red back to The Store, and we started to piece things together," the now older Neville told Rock.

Neville recalled that, from that time on, Red focused on profit. Everything was aimed at making The Store profitable. Red changed Bottomline Billy to full-time rather than part-time bookkeeper. Billy had been Walter's part-time bookkeeper, fitting it in with his apiaristic livelihood. Together Red and Billy cut, pieced, and changed anything that wasn't making a profit.

Red questioned the cost of everything that was done for the Customers.

How much did it cost to

- serve them cocoa on a cold day;
- meet them with umbrellas on a wet day; or
- home deliver for the elderly?

And:

- Did they really need so many people to serve so few Customers?
- Did Customers really mind waiting awhile to be helped?
- Did the Customers really need help in the first place?

Red considered how many staff they could do away with if they made The Store more like a supermarket, only staffing checkouts. Maybe they could have only one inquiry counter or maybe no counter, or staff, at all.

Although the staff protested, Red was convinced that he could save The Store and some of their jobs if he let a few go and changed the way we operated.

The first thing was voluntary redundancies.

"We won't sack people. We'll let the people who want to go, go; no ill will, then." That was, of course, Red's answer even though he was going to change what was a local tradition, an icon of Mullumdabba.

The Store pretty much symbolized everything that Mullumdabba stood for: courtesy, honesty, friendliness, and "doing unto others as you'd have them do unto you."

Red didn't want to upset people. The little boy in him still wanted to be loved.

Of course, pretty much all of the best, most employable staff left. It was only the compulsively loyal or those too old or not talented enough to get another job who stayed.

Next came the Customers themselves.

Red wanted to find out what made them tick. We were given surveys, designed by Bottomline Billy, to determine what the Customers needed, wanted, and desired—what made them happy.

"That in itself wasn't a bad starting place," Neville said. "However, once we had the results back, Red and Billy decided that what the Customers wanted would cost too much, so we thronged to the excitement of a new set of surveys—*not*!

"This time we would determine what would 'satisfy' our Customers. Did we really need to make them *happy*? Surely *satisfied* would be good enough.

"As it turned out, it wasn't that they really needed to be greeted by a cup of hot cocoa on a cold morning to be satisfied. They simply liked it. They would be satisfied with a brief smile. So, cocoa out; smiles in.

"The thing was, we already smiled—when we gave them their cocoa!"

Neville remembered what else they said satisfied them: cheap prices, clean premises, and plenty of stock.

Red's edict came down from what was definitely no longer his father's office: "If that's what satisfies them, then that's what we'll give them."

In response to the protests of the remaining loyal staff (it was only the loyal ones who protested), Red also decreed that "We'll monitor complaints."

"The complaints never came in—and, eventually, neither did the Customers," Neville added.

Dave left. He was due for retirement and, naturally enough, he saw this all coming, so he retired early. He didn't want to "satisfy"

Customers. He did keep in touch with Red, however, and helped as much as he could, between fishing trips.

Upon hearing this information, Rock thanked Neville and said that he had enough to digest for the moment. He retreated to his room to the sounds of Neville's protests: "There's more. Much more. Don't you want to know why? See you tomorrow morning."

In his room Rock ran through the night's events. What did he have so far?

- Walter created a store—The Store—and based it on great service, at a price. Not a price to the Customer; the price was to the company. He'd created a de facto nonprofit organization.

- Red inherited The Store and decided that the path to profitability was to cut costs and keep his Customers "satisfied," monitoring complaints.

- And yes, of course, Red's voluntary redundancy scheme kept him loved by his staff, and he lost some of The Store's best staff (apart from a loyal few).

- And the Customers stayed away in droves. Why? No one complained, other than the few who mentioned missing Dave, who'd now retired, and commented that "There's no one who could ever replace Dave."

Now, back in the real world. What do we know about Customer Complaints?

- Only 5 percent of unhappy Customers complain. 95 percent go away and never come back.
- The average disgruntled Customer tells nine other people. Around 13 percent of disgruntled Customers each tell some twenty other people.

How about Customer Satisfaction?

Is a 95 percent Customer Satisfaction Rate good? What would that mean to your company?

Assume that your company only wants to satisfy Customers:

- If each Customer Service Representative (CSR) serves sixty Customers each day, and they have a 95 percent Customer Satisfaction Rate, then three people may go away unhappy, and they could tell between twenty-seven and sixty people that they were unhappy with the service they received. For each CSR in your company, that means that, in one year, some 15,000 potential Customers could be told that your company doesn't satisfy Customers. If this was the average for a company of, say, thirty-five CSRs, some 500,000 potential Customers per year could be told that your company doesn't satisfy Customers.

And you may never hear a complaint!

Well, then, how would you feel if you had a 99 percent satisfaction rate with your Customers? What does a 99 percent success rate mean?

- In the United States alone,
  - 96 aircraft flying to San Francisco would land at the wrong airport every day;
  - 40,000 babies would be given to the wrong parents every year;
  - 131,000 telephone calls would be misconnected every minute; and
  - 7,458,000 people would get lost on the way to the supermarket every day.

A Note from the Author

From now on, it's your turn to start "reading between the lines." What was the message in this chapter?

Your Action Plan

Quick Tips

1. ....

2. ....

3. ....

Summary

1. ....

2. ....

3. ....

Actions

1. ....

2. ....

3. ....

Chapter 8

STRIKE ONE . . . YOU'RE OUT!

As Rock sorted through his sleep-ridden thoughts, he remembered—the Redhead.

Where was the Redhead?

"She'll be in town awhile." Neville's friendly face peered around the door. "Breakfast in five?"

A veritable flock of gray-haired ex-staff from The Store sat at the tables in the hotel dining room. Rock glanced around. Still no redhead.

"Later. There's plenty of time," chimed in Neville.

"I've told them that you're doing a story—'Redman Folgate: Man or Myth?' Catchy?"

I've heard more original titles in a school magazine, thought Rock.

"I was editor of the *Mullumdabba Mercury* in year 10," Neville proudly boasted, choosing to take Rock's derision as a compliment.

It's marvelous how some people have a perspective that means everything is good, everything is positive, regardless of other people's opinions. They seem to be able to create their own context so that everything is, in fact, positive! Rock was about to straighten Neville out and then thought better of it.

"They each have their own piece of the puzzle," Neville quickly added.

"Take Liz, for instance." A gray-haired woman of seventy-plus stood to greet him. She was elegant and in command, in the manner that only a country woman with five children, six grandchildren, and seven great-grandchildren can be. She no longer wanted or needed to impress. She impressed without effort.

"Elizabeth, to you."

"Elizabeth here was a contemporary of Walter Folgate's. The only one left. She was with The Store from its infancy."

Rock's city ways bounded to the surface with a blunt, "So, Elizabeth, do you think that Redman Folgate killed himself or was killed?"

Elizabeth looked through the abrupt young man. "Neville, I thought you said that there was someone here who wanted to know about the Folgates and The Store? Someone charming and intelligent. Someone that I would enjoy talking with?"

"I thought there was," replied Neville, adding insult to Rock's psychological injury.

Elizabeth walked quietly away to disseminate her wisdom among people of importance—charming, intelligent people. People like the publican's Cattle Dog and Dolly, the bar's mascot.

"Strike one, and you're out. You have absolutely no idea how to treat your Customers, do you?" Neville offered.

"I'm an investigative journalist, not a shop assistant."

"With a bedside manner like that, I wouldn't be surprised if you were here to report on the annual sheep sales.

"Everyone is a Customer. Everyone whom you meet and see and talk to is your Customer."

By now Neville had climbed into the saddle of the bar's replica racehorse. A small plaque swung over his head as he "rode." It had been presented to Walter Folgate by his great friend and protégé, Dr. Jacob Fingle: "To Wally, a mentor, benefactor, and friend, who showed me that I could horse around and still learn!"

Neville continued from atop his steed. "They're all your Customers, because, like every other human being, we're always trying to sell something."

"Never mind Neville. He always jockeys for position in an argument, and this is his favorite topic," a woman consoled Rock, introducing herself to him. "I'm Kerri Faithful."

"Rock Hardstuff. Nice to meet you."

Neville was in full flight now and would be for some time to come. "What is a Customer? Indeed, who are your Customers? Everyone is a Customer—they are, you are, I am. And each and every one of us deserves and desires respect."

Rock resumed. "You knew Redman Folgate?"

"Absolutely. Lovely man . . . eventually."

"How do you mean?"

"Well, it goes back a bit."

Rock glanced at his guide, who was now in full gallop down the far straight of his Customer Service Doctrine.

"I've got time," Rock said, encouraging Neville to tell his story.

Well, not long after Red introduced The New Store— you know, all the 'make more profit, make less people happy' changes—things went downhill. My parents had been Customers and, naturally enough, I became one. All the town was, more or less, satisfied with The New Store. We weren't ecstatic about it. We were 'satisfied.' Or so Red kept telling us.

"As you walked in the front door, there was a sign that verified it, hanging right across Walter's old office:

*Welcome to The New Store. Satisfaction guaranteed,
or your money back**

*subject to conditions

"Young Red was definitely a boy of his word. He really wanted to satisfy his Customers. With every purchase there was a questionnaire, a CSS (Customer Satisfaction Survey) he called it. If you returned ten of them, you were entitled to be put in a drawing to win a dinner for two. Ten lucky shoppers would be taken to a lunch at which Red and Bottomline Billy would talk them through an even more detailed CSS. It was all for our own good, Red insisted. It would help The New Store satisfy us better. Still, he was trying."

With a quick glance toward Neville, Kerri added, "I even remember him saying he wished that he, personally, could replace Dave. And we all knew that the young Red had originally felt that Dave was little more than a curiosity. He was definitely trying."

"The thing was, the surveys had only two categories—satisfied and unsatisfied, and if you put unsatisfied, Red would arrive on your doorstep wanting to know how The New Store could satisfy you. And he was such a nice lad, and everyone felt sorry for all the staff who had stayed with him, so we didn't want to get them into trouble or anything.

"So we were all, pretty much, satisfied," Neville added.

As they were talking, another—you guessed it—gray-haired lady came up to them.

"Reminiscing?" she asked.

"Anne Harris, I'd like you to meet Mr. Hardstuff," Neville said.

"Call me Rock."

"Mr. Hardstuff is a reporter doing a story on The Store."

"Redman Folgate, actually."

"Really," mused Anne, one of the original employees of The New Store. "They're much the same. I heard you mention our wonderful Customer Satisfaction Surveys. Satisfaction, hmm."

Rock prompted her. "You sound reticent."

"More like totally disillusioned! He spent all of his time finding out what satisfied the Customers and totally forgot about us. We were Customers too."

As if on cue, Neville's sermon in the background suddenly came to the foreground. "You have Incoming Customers (they're the ones who buy things from you), Internal Customers (they're the ones you work with), Interpersonal Customers (they're the people in your day-to-day life), and sometimes—sometimes—one person can be two or even three of them, or more. And there's more—at least two more—categories of Customer—"

Oblivious to Neville's interjection, Anne continued. "Redman forgot all about us, so we began to forget about him and, of course, The New Store's Customers. If someone wanted to know where something was, we'd grunt and point—well, not that bad. We wouldn't go out of our way to help them if we were busy, though. Why bother walking them to it, explaining it, and even suggesting a better alternative? They were satisfied if they got the widget that they wanted, and it didn't cost too much. That was satisfaction. Then they finished the road to Wongadoogle."

Rock's ears pricked up. "What has that to do with it?"

"With Wongadoogle only thirty minutes away, everyone had more choices. They could shop somewhere that sold it to them for even less. There were cafés and cinemas, and you could buy fridges and things as well. So why would people shop at The New Store? Satisfaction can be a fleeting thing."

Not to be left out, Kerri threw in, "What was it? Five months, maybe six, and The New Store was—"

"Going downhill fast," said Anne, finishing her story. Bidding Rock farewell with, "See you at the funeral," she simply walked away.

Rock felt that he had very little on the death of Redman Folgate, although he was starting to understand the man behind the name:

- a child who grew up in the shadow of his father
- a father who wasted the family's money by trying to make people happy
- a son who takes over his father's business and tries to make his mark by making it profitable

Was this all a matter of perspective and context? Was Walter blind to economic reality because the people meant so much to him, and was Red equally blind to the people because profitability meant so much to him?

Could this have been the downfall that led to Red's death?

The story so far told Rock that The New Store was basically a disaster. If that was the case, how did Redman become a Customer Service guru and retail entrepreneur worth billions? And why would he kill himself?

When the new road was opened and The New Store died, perhaps—perhaps it was murdered!

Rock was at last onto the makings of a headline story. Images of awards ceremonies, pay raises, and glamorous women filled Rock's mind.

"You've forgotten what Young Red didn't know." Neville shook Rock back to reality.

"Neville, it's been a while. Okay. I'm game. What have I forgotten that Young Red didn't know?"

"People. Young Red didn't know or understand people."

"I know that. Didn't I just say . . . and was Red equally blind to the people because profitability meant so much to him?"

"Well, no."

"Okay, I thought it, though!"

Patiently Neville explained that while Walter may have been blind to the money because he cared about the people, Red might not have been blind to the people. He simply may not have understood people.

Let's look at what you know so far.

Customers—What the heck are they? Who are our Customers?

- Everyone, everywhere.
- Our Customers are Incoming (External), Internal, Interpersonal, and more!
- Incoming Customers are people who call us, e-mail us, or otherwise contact us.
- Internal Customers are people who work with us.
- Interpersonal Customers are our friends, family, and acquaintances.
- Inverse Customers are people whom we buy from—people who serve us.
- (The) In-You Customer: never forget to care for this Customer's needs. We are no more or less important than every other Customer whom we care for.

Your Action Plan

Quick Tips

1. ....

2. ....

3. ....

Summary

1. ....

2. ....

3. ....

Actions

1. ....

2. ....

3. ....

CHAPTER 9

THE BEGINNING OF THE END
OF THE BEGINNING

For two years Red had lobbied to get the road improved between Mullumdabba and Wongadoogle. It was regularly written in the Any Other Comments box on his Customer Satisfaction Surveys. He genuinely wanted to satisfy his Customers, even if it had nothing to do with his Pride and Joy, The New Store. ("Pride" was the name of his premises in Mullumdabba; "Joy" was still only a dream, which would be his new New Store in the city one day.)

Red had managed to get a place on the Planning Committee, and his vote was to be the deciding vote for the road-funding application. A resounding cheer went through the council chambers. The Wongadoogle/Mullumdabba road would become all-weather, a perfect road, except for the insects that resided in the roadside grass. A jar of Bug Off! was a small price to pay for civilization. And maybe, just maybe, Wongadoogle people would hear about The New Store's satisfaction guarantee and Joy would become a reality.

That was six months ago. The road was now open, and the profits were down. "Why is no one shopping here anymore? Aren't my Customers satisfied?" The questions spun through Red's head.

He'd even repainted and renovated The New Store. Still, the profits declined. Did Pride really come before a fall? In Mullumdabba, most definitely.

He'd let go of staff. Oddly enough, they didn't seem to mind. And, very soon, they all had very good jobs in Wongadoogle!

What was going wrong? Were his surveys faulty?

He would have asked Bottomline Billy, except Billy had resigned and moved to Wongadoogle.

There was still enough of a profit margin to keep The New Store open. That was only because his father had owned Pride long before Red took over, so there was no mortgage. The townsfolk hadn't deserted him completely. They just found their satisfaction elsewhere. Someplace where several aspects of their needs could be satisfied at one time. Someplace that gave them more than simply extra services and facilities—a bigger town. How could Red compete with that?

"At least that was the way it was told to me by my mother." Rock had been cornered by Bruce Metcalfe, son of Rita Metcalfe, one of the last of Walter's original staff to be let go by Red.

"What did he do to get things back on track?" Rock asked.

"Well, the story goes that Red had received yet another letter from City & Country Discounters. They'd buy The New Store, though not for as much as before. They knew things were on the decline, so why would they pay more than they needed to? Young Red would still come out ahead. Just."

Bruce recalled the story he knew that Red had needed to think, and he'd chipped a molar. He'd thought that a drive to the dentist in Wongadoogle might help.

At the very least, one of the pains would go away!

So off he went, along the new road that he was responsible for and that was, likewise, responsible for his downfall. His mind was distracted, so he hadn't filled his car before he left. As the gas gauge approached zero, he could see himself sitting at the side of the road, with a toothache, waiting for a passerby to pick him up. Clearly, there'd be plenty of passersby, mainly his former satisfied Customers on their way to shop in Wongadoogle.

The idea of running out of petrol and sitting by the side of the road didn't seem so bad when he compared it to nursing his broken molar as he chitchatted with a Customer who had deserted him. Then, as if from nowhere, he saw a sign for a fuel station—a sign he'd never noticed before.

He turned off, and a few moments later he was pulling into the station as his car coughed its last ethanol breath. No sooner had he stopped than a young redheaded boy was at his door.

"How much would you like?" the boy asked

Surprised, Red sat dumbfounded.

"Shall I fill it for you? Or would you just like enough to get you to a cheaper station? We're in the middle of nowhere, so it costs a bit extra to get our fuel here. Sorry that we can't sell it for any less. Twenty dollars would get you to town, where it's cheaper."

Still dumbfounded, this time by the boy's honesty, Red managed to splutter, "A full tank would be great."

"Cheers," said the eager young man as three more boys came out, every one a freckled redhead: one for the tires, one for the mirrors and windows, and one was learning, so he chatted to Red to pass his Customer's time as the first boy fueled the car.

Reacting to Red's shocked and stressed look, the "small talker" said, "Washroom's at the back. No need for a key. Anyone can use it."

Red took the directions and smiled as he walked past an older redheaded man sitting and watching the lads work—their father, he assumed. Then Red entered the most amazing washroom. A fuel station washroom that was pristine—it even smelled good. What was that . . . lavender? Yes, lavender-scented oil misted from the wall to his right. The pale-blue tiles sparkled, and the granitelike walls shone. As he looked up from splashing his face, the mirror even somehow managed to make him look young and happy. He looked great and felt great—confused yet great!

To complete his experience, there was a choice of hand-drying options: paper towel, blower, fabric, or ray lamp.

As he returned to his car after drying his hands, Red was approached by the dad, who said, "You happy with the kids?"

"Absolutely."

"An' the washroom?"

Still a little dumbfounded, Red stuttered, "Yes . . . great . . . yes . . ."

"Washroom's a place for washin'. Washin's gotta be clean, else you come out dirty an' it ain't worth the effort."

The small talker handed Red a glass of iced water. "Lot of dust in the air this time of year."

"An' insects," the windscreen boy added.

Red handed the glass back, noting that his mirrors sparkled with that same "make you look and feel great" sheen. Small, precise arcs swept across Red's windscreen. And, as a finishing touch, the boy carefully removed a trapped butterfly from the wipers and set it free.

"No need to kill things, I reckon." His cap slipped, and a cascade of long, thick red hair erupted over his—or rather, her—shoulders. Their eyes met, and time stopped.

The butterfly slowly alighted, and she smiled at Red. "Thanks for being our Customer and letting me be yours," she said, and suddenly only the boy with the credit card machine remained.

Red no longer needed to go to town. His tooth was fine. In fact, *he* was fine. Everything was just . . . great. Red now realized that he was a Customer, and so too was everyone else.

From that time on, The New Store changed. All the signs saying The New Store reverted to The Store, and the satisfaction guaranteed banners were replaced by ones that said things like:

> *Tell us what you want, and we'll do more.*

> *If we don't make you happy, don't tell your friends . . .*
> *tell us!*

> *Excellence is not an option. It's our obligation—and*
> *our pleasure.*

Red changed the surveys, and there were fewer of them. Often he'd simply walk up and ask Customers, "Did you enjoy shopping with us?" and eventually, "Did we give you excellent service today? Did we make you happy today? How could we make you even happier next time?"

Red started personally greeting people in The Store with words like, "Hi, I'm Redman Folgate. I'm responsible for The Store," "Thank you for being our Customer. We really care about making you happy," and, "How about helping us make you even happier?"

Sometimes he'd even put on a disguise and use his middle name, imagining that the Customers' responses would be more candid.

A lot of people felt that Young Red had done his usual trick and gone to the extreme yet again. Slowly things and people adapted, and it became apparent to everyone that Red genuinely did feel that he was everyone's Customer and that everyone was his. And he really did care.

He included his staff in this new approach. They were all his Customers, and he was theirs. He cared, and soon they did too. In fact, it wasn't long before people were asking to work for The Store, and people from Wongadoogle and further afield were driving along the road that Red had built to come to shop in Mullumdabba.

In fact, as the story goes, that fuel station made a killing, with all the extra traffic, and the redheaded girl ended up going to university and beyond.

Oh, yes. And Red, well, people in town got to calling him Mr. Customer Service.

What made the new The Store so special?

- Working at The Store became more akin to working in the hospitality industry than working in sales.
- The sales team had become purchase facilitators, rather than sales reps. They didn't sell products, they *helped* their Customers *buy* products.
- The Store sold *service* first, *products* second.
- The Store didn't have Customer Service Representatives (CSRs); it had Customer Experts (CEs).
- They all approached Customer Service as "We care about our Customers and treat them as we like to be treated when we're Customers, or even better!"
- Happiness soon became a measure of success for everyone.

Your Action Plan

Quick Tips

1. ....

2. ....

3. ....

Summary

1. ....

2. ....

3. ....

Actions

1. ....

2. ....

3. ....

CHAPTER 10

THE NEW STORE BECOMES
THE OLD STORE, ANEW

Once he had pulled his thoughts together, Rock wanted to know where he should go from there. Naturally enough Neville had something to say.

Neville explained, with renewed vigor, the new Store became everything that the original Store had been, and more. This time it had a new leader; "Young Red" no longer existed. The new Store was captained by Redman Folgate, a man of vision, a man on a mission. From now on, Redman would be his own best Customer.

No longer would he be satisfied with "satisfaction." Anything that wasn't good enough for him, wasn't good enough for anyone else—internal and external Customers alike.

"When we met a Customer's expectations, we were asked, 'Why? Why did you only meet their expectations?' 'How do you feel when your expectations are merely met?' and 'How do you feel when your expectations are exceeded?' not a bad set of questions for anyone to ask themselves, anytime and under any circumstances," Neville said.

He also recounted that Redman returned to what he called "the Fuel Station of the Epiphany" (FSE) every week to fill up his car and his mind, even though it was the most expensive fuel in the district. He loved the station's service, and it reminded him of what was important—people.

Julia, the redheaded attendant with the thing for butterflies— Redman had asked her father what her name was—had gone to boarding school, then university, and then she was traveling.

Old Dad Johnson and Redman became firm friends over the years that Redman frequented the FSE. Still, Redman looked for Julia every time just in case.

Redman would regularly pick Dad Johnson's brain or use him as a sounding board. After all, he had Customer Service right long before Redman even thought about it!

Eventually Redman had to ask, "How did you know what to do to make your Customers happy?"

"Well, it was hard," the old sage replied sarcastically. "I put myself in their place. I thought to myself, *What would I like to happen when I drive in to a fuel station?* Then, *pow!* I suddenly had an idea of what would make them happy."

"Great. I already do that," prodded Redman. "It works for general Customers whom you sell things to. What about all the other people you deal with? Everyone loves you."

"I use the Three Prompts."

Redman looked puzzled.

At this stage, Neville interrupted his story, saying to Rock, "You look about as puzzled as Redman did."

Rock's frustration at the prolonged storytelling of the town of gray-haired troubadours could be contained no longer. "Three Prompts. Great fuel stations. Old men and a billionaire nicknamed Mr. Customer Service. I just can't see how this helps me work out what happened to Redman Folgate. What I want to know is who would have wanted to kill Folgate, or at the very least why he was found dead last week?"

"From the city, aren't you?" Neville replied from his leisurely position, lounging in the hotel's best armchair, feet on the hotel's "one but best" table.

"Yes, I—"

"It was rhetorical. That means that I already know the answer, so you don't need to answer it. Have you ever noticed how so much of what we say is so completely obvious? Things like, 'It's hot,' 'It's dry,' 'Try not to get run over.' We want our Customers to keep coming back to us."

As Neville commenced to explain his philosophy of language, his foot slipped from the table, and his shin hit the edge with a *crack*.

"That's got to hurt," Rock consoled sarcastically.

"That's exactly what I mean," said Neville adamantly, proving his point. "You'll need to understand language to understand Redman."

"I'm a journalist."

"I'm glad that you can admit your shortcomings; it's the first step to recovery. More on that later. For now, the Three Prompts.

"The prompts were developed to prompt us to think and act— to get us to ask ourselves key questions before and after we deal with people, most particularly before. We tended to use them after the event only if things didn't work out quite the way we would have liked them to so that we could learn from the challenges that we'd faced.

"In the old days, around the new millennium, people referred to 'win-win situations.' That became pretty hackneyed, because what they really meant was, 'I want to win this situation, and if I need to help my opponent win so that I can win, then I will.'

"As you can see, it wasn't really as altruistic as it first seemed.

"'Win-win' was an adversarial contest. After all, how can anyone win unless there's some form of contest? It often involved manipulative techniques taught by sales or negotiation gurus. There were technique experts and countertechnique experts and countercountertechnique experts. Some of the historical texts of the time even quote one expert's technique and tell you how to identify which expert devised it and then how to counter it with another expert's technique.

"A whole industry of speakers and trainers developed to teach people how to win in a win-win situation—that is, how you can win more than your opponent wins."

Neville explained that these experts based their efforts on the following questions:

1) What do they (my opponents) want?
2) What do I want?
3) How do I get more than them while making them feel like they got more than me?

"The first two of these prompts are quite valid," Neville said. "However, they forgot a basic precept of human interaction—enjoyment."

Rock looked at Neville incredulously.

"Okay. And sex. Where I come from, that's enjoyable!"

Now, at last, he really had Rock's attention. It's amazing how the right small word can grab someone's ear when a whole dictionary of long ones can't.

Neville continued. "People had forgotten to enjoy themselves. Sure, you might both win in a win-win situation, and you might enjoy the winning. Although, if that's all you get from it, it's highly unlikely that the two of you will choose to go head-to-head all over again, unless you really have to.

"So our third prompt related to the enjoyment of the journey, not simply the outcome. It was:

3) How do I help both of us enjoy getting there?

"Not only does it encourage us to find an enjoyable route, it also reminds us that every Customer Transaction that we have, with every kind of Customer, is a journey of some kind. We both start somewhere and both want to go somewhere else.

"So, our Three Prompts were:

1) What do they (Our Customers) want?
2) What do I want?
3) How can I help both of us enjoy getting there?

Neville said that this is how Dad Johnson explained it to Red: "You see, if you don't enjoy what you're doing, how can anyone around you enjoy it? And isn't that what life's all about—enjoyment? Our Customers enjoy feeling special, and we enjoy helping them feel special. If we appreciate them, it's only natural that they'll appreciate us.

"Think about it. Don't we love people because they love us? Sure, there are times when we think that we love someone who doesn't love us. Question is, 'Do we really love them? Or love them enough?'

"Take Julia, for instance. Even though you've hardly seen her, the minute your eyes met through the windshield, there was something. She loves you, and you love her, even though you've hardly spoken.

"Now if there were two women who you thought you loved—and yes, people tell me it does happen, and not just at the Cineplex—who do you think you'd ultimately end up with and love the most? The one who didn't love you or the one who did love you—loved you with all her heart? Like Julia."

Somehow most of this message hadn't sunk into Red's mind. It had frozen shut with, "Take Julia, for instance. Even though you've hardly seen her, the minute your eyes met through the windshield, there was something. She loves you."

The rest of the sentence, "you love her, even though you've hardly spoken," was blatantly obvious to Redman. He knew that. The new information was what had caused a short circuit in his mind: "She loves you."

If that was the case, why was she at university? Why wasn't she at his side?

At that moment, Julia walked in, grabbed Red, kissed him, and simultaneously presented Dad Johnson with her degree in psychology.

From that moment on, Red and Julia were inseparable.

"Or so the story goes," Neville added. "Okay, maybe it wasn't quite so dramatic. You're a journalist. You admitted it, remember? You know not to let the truth get in the way of a good story!"

Rock pondered aloud. "That's how Redman and Julia met?"

"Absolutely, without a lie. Well, it was pretty close to that. Her Dad did own a fuel station, and Red did go there a lot, and she did go to university . . ."

Rock thought this through, trying desperately to find an angle. The Store was a major success by the time Redman and Julia were married. A headline flashed through Rock's mind: "Fuel Station Owner's Daughter Catches Billionaire in Tender Trap."

Neville picked up his story, choosing politely to ignore Rock's search for a suitable tabloid headline. "The Store was only just getting back on its feet. Julia was part of the driving force behind its resurgence, using her father's principles, the Three Prompts. Together they expanded The Store, nationally and then internationally. The Store fought the trends for e-commerce—e-mail, e-chats, e-catalogues, e-shopping, e-enterprise . . . "e" in general. Redman and Julia recognized that, as society became more affluent, the value we place on the dollar price for an item would become less, and the value we place on being respected and treated as worthwhile and important would become greater.

"Much to the distaste of the major E-Nterprise retail Web portals, the concept of personalized Customer Service Excellence began to take hold. People—people with money—really did prefer the face-to-face experience, as long as it was convenient, pleasant, and predictable. People, real people, liked to be served by other real people.

"This was The Store's approach—providing a personalized excellent Customer Service experience. Wherever you were in the world, you could walk into The Store, and you would know what would be there and that you would have a great time buying it because of reliable product lines, reasonable prices, and predictably pleasant staff, who even used a common terminology and provided an uncommonly excellent level of Customer Service.

"The Store really began to turn the tables on companies that thought people only wanted the cheapest prices."

There had to be an "angle", so Rock dug deeper into his psyche.

*   *   *

What had he just learned?

A moral, perhaps? Find someone who does what you want to do and does it *very* well. Then learn from him or her. Mentors and role models can be of great value and great fun.

What about the three Customer Service prompts?

1) What do they want?
2) What do I want?
3) How do I help both of us *enjoy* getting there?

What do they want?

- A product
- Information
- What else (in three words or less)?
- reassurance
- satisfaction
- empowerment
- guidance
- choices
- to vent
- to impress
- . . . and a myriad of other things that are subsets of these

What do I want?

- to exceed expectations (my Customer's and my own)
- to increase my excellence ratings
- to increase my sales margin
- to expand my knowledge
- fulfillment (my Customer's and my own)
- enjoyment (my Customer's and my own)
- to surprise myself

How do I help both of us *enjoy* getting there?
There are two basic steps to this.

a) How do I help both of us get there?: To achieve this, there is a vast skill set of Customer Service techniques and tools that can be used to assist in satisfying your Customer.

b) How do we both *enjoy* the process?: To get *enjoyment* you need to
   - answer the challenge of personalizing each conversation to the unique, individual needs of each Customer;
   - find specific aspects of Customer Service that genuinely appeal to you;
   - compliment and complement your Customer; and
   - smile, and maybe even laugh, with your Customer.

Your Action Plan

Quick Tips

1. ....

2. ....

3. ....

Summary

1. ....

2. ....

3. ....

Actions

1. ....

2. ....

3. ....

CHAPTER 11

GROWTH

To the sound of the returning rain, Rock sat in his room dredging through his notes. Who were the suspects?

Neville—now he always had something to say, and it really was quite irritating the way he answered questions that you hadn't asked yet. Could he have any possible motive?

Means, motive, and opportunity—that's what Rock needed.

Rock searched the Internet intermittently, not because of a limit on his time but because the service on what he now knew to be his outmoded TeleTetxa WC350D continued to be sporadic due to the weather.

He found a brief article on Folgate's cause of death—poison. At this stage, police were uncertain whether it had been self-administered. They simply stated that investigations were underway and were being overseen by the renowned Dr. Jacob Fingle. If Rock waited too long, it would all be old news, not the breaking news that he'd imagined. The article also mentioned the type of poison—Boreumdextrapropalene. What the heck was that?

His next search confused him even more.

The facts on *E-Ncyclopedia* read:

> Boreumdextrapropalene—a poison. Usually acquired through the distilling of royal jelly in combination with polypropalene by-products and a drenching agent. It was commonly a concern in the twentieth century when plastics were in common use as storage containers and bees were kept on farms with other animals.
>
> It can kill you or at least make you very, very sick, in a manner similar to that of tetrodotoxin, the "zombie poison." Even then it might kill you, just as you think that you're getting better. Or it could kill you and then, just when you decide that you are happy to be dead, you might wake up, after experiencing all the symptoms of being dead!
>
> For further information see the e-book *Poison: Things That Might Kill You, or at Least Make You Very, Very Sick*, written by Fredrick Bee, published by City and Country E-Press, a division of City & Country E-Nterprises.

Who else could I consider? Rock asked himself. *Anne Harris, shop assistant; Kerri Faithful, Customer; Max Howard, another shop assistant; Bottomline Bill—sorry, Bottomley—bookkeeper . . .*
Then of course there were Julia and Old Dad Johnson.
I don't even know who is still alive, let alone who had something to gain by Redman's death.
Hang on, I'm missing something. What should I remember that I don't? I don't remember what I should remember. I don't even remember the . . . the . . . I don't even remember what . . .
Rock extricated himself from the impending spiral dive of an information void.

He needed sleep—a long, secure, quiet, peaceful sleep. He thought through the day's efforts. The headline for "Who Killed Redman Folgate?" still eluded him. All that he could think of was "The Three Prompts and Questions about Who Customers Are."

He began to count sheep, only that reminded him of his other work. Still, it was boring enough to distract his mind sufficiently for one rogue image to enter—an image from a dream that would not surface for days to come.

*   *   *

A Note from the Author

Hi.

Given that you have made it this far, I'd like to thank you for reading this book. I realize that it may all seem a tad confusing at present, but wait, there's more.

To help you along the way, I thought that a summary—the story so far—might help.

We've established who Redman Folgate is and what his store—The Store—stands for: amazing Customer Service, service so good that it doesn't simply satisfy a Customer's needs and wants, it looks to his or her desires and continually exceeds his or her expectations.

We've seen what happened to The Store when it guaranteed satisfaction, but only satisfaction. In today's world we need to do more, much more than simply satisfy our Customers. There are millions of people out there who can satisfy your Customers' needs, and e-commerce is making our world much smaller and exposing what had formerly been local or personal markets to competitors from all over the world. And many other countries have much lower overhead than we do, so they can deliver a lower price for virtually any product.

In today's world thousands of people sell what you do. You can't stay in business and remain just one of the sheep in a flock. To remain at the top, you must have an edge, which may be many things. One of the most important (and affordable) differentiating edges is Customer Service Excellence—Customer Service that is beyond anything your Customers can ever get from a discounter.

To survive in the modern world, as Redman Folgate put it, "Excellence is not an option; it is our obligation and our pleasure . . . and our life's blood." Hand in hand with this obligation is the responsibility to keep developing and improving your Customer Service Excellence, because as soon as you have set the playing field, one of your competitors will move the goal posts. Always make your competitors run uphill and into the sun! Or better yet, ensure that you are so far ahead of everyone else that you have no competitors!

In case you've lost the focus of the story, that's what this book is all about!

The principles contained herein apply to everyone. Feel free to use them in the following situations:

- in a retail environment
- in the office

- while negotiating with a government or your spouse, parents, or children

The principles are the same—it's only the context that changes. *So, that said, let's wake up Rock again!*

CHAPTER 12

ROCK WAKES UP, AGAIN

There they were, a flock of sheep standing upright doing an ancient soft-shoe routine, each one wearing an old top hat. Seated in the audience, one lone ram surveyed the chorus line, seeking its perfect mate. Suddenly they all froze. "Baa Brand Pure Newe Wool—straight off the sheep's back" was emblazoned on a banner above them. Their images were slowly replaced by a voice announcing, "This interruption to your sheep is brought to you by City and Country E-Nterprises—satisfying customers for a century. Sweet dreams!"

Rock shouted as he jumped from his bed. "They dumped my last story. If I don't nail Folgate's death, I'm destitute."

A knock bounced happily off Rock's door.

"Come in, Neville."

"You ready to solve the mystery now?"

Rock stood silent—stunned. Was Neville really going to reveal a genuine lead to him? "If there's one thing Redman used to say . . ."

No, he wasn't, realized Rock.

". . . . I heard that! What do you want from me? I'm introducing you to everyone who, knew and loved Red!"

"That's exactly it! People who knew and loved Red wouldn't be the people who killed him. Nothing I've heard so far does more than give me background."

Neville returned to his story. "Let me ask you three questions that Red would ask anyone who wanted to find out something about a Customer—and remember that a Customer is virtually anyone you meet, want to meet, or have met. Red would say—"

Rock was tiring of this Customer Service game. "I know. What do they want? What do I want? And how do I help both of us enjoy getting there?"

"Well that too," added Neville. "I was more thinking about information gathering. How many ears do you have?"

"Two," Rock dutifully replied.

"How many eyes do you have?"

Again Rock humored Neville; he was, after all, the only person in town who showed any real interest in what he was doing.

"Two."

"How many mouths do you have?"

"Aah, trick question? You thought I'd say two! One."

"Exactly. One," said Neville triumphantly. "So why do you talk so much? Today, listen. Really listen. And I don't mean just to the words. You did that yesterday. Listen to everything, and look at everything too. Okay, let's make that even clearer. Do more than just look . . . see! Then you'll have your answers," he added as he ducked out the door. "Breakfast in five?"

And he was gone!

Damn. Caught again by a small-town hick. Rock thought. Maybe Neville was right. Was there something that he'd been missing?

Okay. Today I'll listen—really listen!

"And see things too." Neville's voice echoed up the stairwell.

Rock also decided to take the rest of Neville's advice— "Breakfast in five!"

Listening would be much easier on a full stomach.

*   *   *

Right then—what did Rock know about listening—really listening?

How many ears do you have?

How many eyes do you have?

How many mouths do you have?

Then why do we talk so much?

At The Store they aimed to listen at least 70 percent of the time and talk no more than 30 percent of the time.

And that meant listen—really listen.

They listened to

- the words that their Customer used, to help them understand and anticipate their Customers' needs;
- the Customer's tone and rhythm, to help them understand their Customers' desires and emotional state; and

- their our own voice, to ensure that they were smiling, friendly, respectful, and giving excellent Customer Service.

Then they continued to listen to all aspects of their Customer's voice so that they were aware of any change in their Customer's needs, desires, or emotional state.

Your Action Plan

Quick Tips

1. ....

2. ....

3. ....

Summary

1. ....

2. ....

3. ....

Actions

1. ....

2. ....

3. ....

CHAPTER 13

ROCK TRIES TO LISTEN

Rock reluctantly examined his breakfast: chops, hash browns, gravy, and pancakes. He was sure that he'd asked whether they served Lamb Liver (known to the locals as "fry").

"Liver isn't on today's menu," Neville consoled him. "If you don't like the pork chops, you can have something else. The bacon's great," Neville added between sumptuous mouthfuls.

"It's fine. I just . . . so who do I talk to?" Then, playing off Neville's reaction "Sorry. Who do I listen to today?"

"I thought that it might be worth seeing and hearing what Chris Paterson has to say."

"Never heard of him."

Walking Rock to a corner of the hotel lounge—"Her. She was one of the first outsiders to work with Red once he began to review his approach to Customer Service Excellence. She knew a lot about a little. And the little she knew about was a lot!"

Rock winced. He could feel a paradox coming on, and they always gave him such a headache.

Sitting quietly in the corner of the lounge was a small woman who had clearly been extremely fetching in her younger days. She was quietly sipping an early-morning Singapore Sling. As they approached, she raised her china-blue eyes, mesmerizing Rock and bringing Neville to a halt by his side.

After a pause worthy of a formerly world-renowned opera singer, now an aged dowager waiting for her audience to recognize her, Christina spoke to Neville. "This is he?"

"Yes. He this is!" replied Neville.

Christina smiled one of those warm, friendly, seductive smiles. "Good. So pleased to meet you, Rock."

Neville jarred Rock out of his trance. "She's pleased to meet you."

"And I, her." Rock, at this stage, found it interesting to note that both he and Neville had immediately adopted Christina's peculiarly formal, almost artificially royal, language pattern. Was this part of an "empathizing process" which he had learned from Neville?

"Nope. I didn't teach you this. Could be we're both smitten," he whispered to Rock. "I've been for years."

Rock looked at Neville and then at Christina. She was far too old for him, or so he tried to tell himself. Still, there was something about her.

"So, you'd like to know about Redman Folgate. I can understand that." Her comment was met with a resounding silence, so Christina tantalized them further with that smile. "Now, tell me how I can help you."

Rock hesitated, glanced at Neville, and then replied, "I'd like to understand Folgate. I'd like to know what he knew."

"That's a tall order. Let me see what I can do to help you. What exactly would you like me to do for you?"

Her question hung in the air as Rock momentarily weighed whether he could ask for what he really wanted. She was older than his usual fantasy, but she was unlike anyone he had ever met.

Her words continued to hang in the air as she moved closer to Rock and added, "Fantastic. I know what I can do to help you, Rock. I find you quite intriguing. I'm amazed that I hadn't noticed you before. You can't have been here long . . . What brings you to our quiet, little town?"

Flattered, Rock took the bait. "I was here to report on the end-of-year sheep sales."

"Really?"

"I travel throughout the country reporting on developments in the rural sector."

"All over the country . . . ?" She had the ability to add a question mark to silence, gently prompting you to continue.

"Absolutely. I've been a reporter for nearly ten years." A nod of acknowledgment, and Rock was well on his way to telling his life story.

"I grew up in the country, so it seemed natural to write about country issues. I've always been intrigued by people—what they do, why, and how."

Christina had Rock in full flight now. All he needed was a gentle nudge here and there to guide him. "And you're keen to hear about Red . . ." She waited for him to fill in the pause. "Because . . . you . . . ?"

"I think that there's a great story in it. Who he was, what he did . . . Like I said, I'm intrigued by people."

Not satisfied, Christina artfully redirected Rock's responses. "I love ambition in a man. I would have imagined that rural reporting would be a bit limiting for someone as intelligent and capable as you."

"I've often thought that I was wasted."

"Rock, I would have thought that you'd make a great investigative journalist. A reporter just reports. I'm sure that you do so much more than that. Yes?"

"Absolutely. I pride myself on interpreting the news. Even sheep prices—I can see the trends, and I know the reasons for a slump or a boom."

Neville sat amazed and amused as Rock divulged the workings of his mind for the next hour; loss of rank to rural reporting, conspiracies, suspicions, unrequited love and mistakes made, and yet to make.

Christina subtly brought the interview to a close with a glance at her watch, adding, "Thank you so much, Rock. It's been a real pleasure. Have you got everything that you need?"

"Absolutely."

She pecked him on the cheek and drifted out of the room.

After a minute or two, Neville broke the silence. "So was that as good for you as it was for her?"

"Great. I have absolutely . . ." Rock glanced at his notepad. "Nothing! . . . I . . . how . . ."

Nothing? That was the first thing that Rock had done wrong today.

"Christina gives great Customer Service. Except for one thing. You didn't really get what you thought you wanted. You did enjoy it, though, didn't you?"

As his mind began to open, Rock summed up his feelings: "It was as though she knew the Three Prompts and only used the last two."

Neville picked up on the point. "She got what she wanted, and you both enjoyed the journey. Darn it. I even enjoyed the journey as an observer."

"She did more than that. She used a whole basket of tricks," Rock added angrily, feeling cheated.

"Not tricks. Christina is simply a master of what she does. No tricks there. Just some very helpful tools."

Looking at his empty notebook and thinking back, Rock added, "There was a lot more than basic Customer Service there."

"If you look carefully enough, you'll see that you did get what you really wanted. However, learning to listen may take a bit more work."

* * *

Let's look at what Christina she did.

What "Tools" Did Christina Use?

- She used the Customer's name.
- She smiled; it really could be heard in her voice.
- She established the other person's needs and desires—what they wanted, why, and how? (In Rock's case, he wanted to impress a pretty woman and to talk about himself.)
- She listened actively, prompting the conversation with cues, acknowledgments, and subtle moments of silence. She even placed "silent question marks" among her words.
- She showed genuine interest.
- She used positives and personals, "fantastic" and "excellent."
- She used I4U statements like "What *I* could do *for you* is . . ."

Your Action Plan

Quick Tips

1. ....

2. ....

3. ....

Summary

1. ....

2. ....

3. ....

Actions

1. ....

2. ....

3. ....

CHAPTER 14

CUSTOMER SERVICE ZEN

Rock licked his wounds and felt sorry for himself as Neville arranged another meeting.

This time Rock would be prepared. He dug frantically through his notes, not the notes that he hadn't taken during his encounter with Christina, but rather his notes from previous meetings and discussions.

He'd clearly learned from Christina that someone could use the basic Customer Service tools in almost any situation, and this time he'd come away with the information that he wanted, and the other person would be left wanting. He was going to be a winner this time!

Neville interrupted. "That's not what was meant. Christina used her skills on you so you'd have a reason to clearly remember them—to use, not abuse, them. Only then can you start to understand Redman."

Bouncing off Rock's blank expression, he said, "I know it sounds a bit Zen. But by experiencing these tools as a negative, you can now place yourself in a better position to apply them positively so that everyone benefits."

After a interminable pause where neither man would accept the silent prompt of the other, Rock acquiesced. "Okay. I have Christina's weapons under my belt. So I'm going into the next battle fully armed?"

"It's not a battle. You now have skills and tools, not weapons."

"From your side, maybe."

At that, Neville rose from his seat and walked out the door.

That appeared to be the second wrong thing that Rock had done today!

Rock sat alone, dumbstruck. If he was going to be dumbstruck, he thought, he'd best be in his own room. There's nothing worse than being dumbstruck in a public place.

In reality there are a lot of things worse than being dumbstruck in a public place; it's just that Rock couldn't think of any in his current state of dumbstruckedness. But time would tell!

So, dumbstruckedly, Rock returned to his room and sat quietly, contemplatively, until he realized that he was sitting almost monklike. Then he just sat quietly, thinking.

In the ensuing silence, Rock found himself with time on his hands—the WC350N Wrist Communicator was, once again, malfunctioning, projecting the time directly onto the back of his hand. He shook the contrary device and received a message: "Thank you for contacting TeleTexta E-Communication, a division of City & Country E-Nterprises, satisfying customers for a century.

The video footage that you have recorded has been downloaded to City & Country E-Nterprises and will be reviewed in due course."

Rock didn't even know that he could record video footage, let alone that he had sent it to City & Country. "I wonder what I sent them?" went through his mind. Then he went back to his self-pitying silence.

That was the third thing that Rock had done wrong today.

No sooner had he thought that than there was a quiet knock on his door.

"So, back for more punishment, eh? I'm sorry, Neville, though I don't know what for. Come in. It's open."

That was the fourth thing that Rock had done wrong today. And normally three things are more than enough for anyone to do wrong (in one day).

* * *

Neville knocked on Rock's door. Just one knock.

Time had given both of them an opportunity to reflect on the past couple of days.

After all, Rock was Neville's Customer, and Neville should practice what he preached. It was only fair. And Rock was pretty new to this.

While everyone in Mullumdabba had grown up with the concept of Service Excellence, Rock was city folk. Or worse, country folk who preferred the city. Neville never really got the hang of such people! It was a bit like Wednesdays. He could never really get the hang of those either.

Still, they did exist, and Neville knew that other types of people probably existed that he might never really get the hang of either. What always amazed Neville was how, even with so many different types of people, there were still so many people that were the same.

He knocked again. That was the second time that Neville had knocked today.

Still no answer—was Rock asleep? Sulking? More likely sulking. A third knock; give him a chance. In the shower, perhaps?

Maybe. Just maybe, Rock had . . . with the impetuous fourth knock, the door slowly swung open.

Now, that was the fourth knock. And normally three knocks are more than enough for anyone, though today was a Wednesday, of course!

Rock's room was empty. Well, not empty. There was a single bed, a small bedside table, a dressing table, and a mirror. Really, for a room that appeared at first to be empty, there was quite a lot in it. Neville pondered the way that people often said rather silly things like, "The room's empty," when quite clearly it wasn't!

But there was obviously something important missing from the room—Rock.

Your Action Plan

Quick Tips

1. ....

2. ....

3. ....

Summary

1. ....

2. ....

3. ....

Actions

1. ....

2. ....

3. ....

CHAPTER 15

THERE ARE WORSE THINGS

Rock strained to open his eyes. His head ached like it had been hit by a baseball bat wrapped in wool. As his blurred vision gradually restored itself, after several momentary hallucinations about rolling seas, or were they *C*s . . . seas of *C*s breaking on oceans of sand, one *C*, then another, and another—nothing except *C*s and more *C*s.

Rock shook some sense into his head, which clearly wasn't the most sensible thing to do; it immediately felt as though it would fall off. Or at least it made Rock wish that it would.

He began to take in his surroundings. He was in a hot, dry shearing shed. The sun beat through missing slats in the roof, and star-like dust danced in the shards of light. It would have been quite beautiful if it hadn't been for the intense heat of the sun on Rock's face.

References to holes in the ozone layer had long ceased around here. People referred, instead, to those rare instances when the ozone layer could briefly be identified.

Dirt mixed easily with the decades of lanolin produced by the wool, and the shed's odor was reminiscent of the inside of a well-loved Ugg boot. Grit and dust clung to everything, and Rock was dumbstruck (*Old habits die hard,* he thought).

Then he was briefly un-dumbstruck as he realized that there was, in fact, something worse than being dumbstruck in a public place and that this was it—being dumbstruck in a very un-public place, somewhere like an abandoned shearing shed at noon, in the middle of nowhere in the middle of summer, tide up, and with nothing to drink.

As his mind pondered and wandered, he thought through all the things that had led to this moment. At least he thought that he'd thought of all the things that had led to this moment. As he couldn't understand why he was here, he had probably missed something.

As he sat there, puzzled, his mind stopped, and he was dumbstruck yet again. He heard footsteps, and then it struck him—not an idea, the wool covered baseball bat again.

Rock's world went gray.

*   *   *

As Neville turned to leave the empty room, his foot got stuck in an oily splotch, and as he bent down to examine it, his eyes were attracted to a thread of wool that swung provocatively from the bottom of the bedspread.

Even with Neville's remarkable imagination, he couldn't think of any reason that Rock would have this wool. "Pure Newe wool." No one around here used "Pure Newe wool"; it was shorn in late autumn, and that left the sheep with no wool in the winter, which was very nasty in these parts.

And the sticky stuff?

Neville's world went gray to the words "came back for my wool and lanolin."

*　　*　　*

Rock's world gradually ungrayed.

As the shed came into focus, he realized that he hadn't been dreaming. There was indeed a large lump on his head and a correspondingly large ache in his brain.

The shed was the same, only darker than before. Something else was different too. He was marginally more comfortable than before. There was a slight cushioning between his body and the floor.

He nudged the lumpy cushion.

Not bad, he thought. Definitely better than before. *How nice*, he thought, *courtesy among thieves*, although that would mean that he was a thief. So he reformulated the thought, this time simply thinking, *How nice*.

Rock's hands were now tied in front of him, another more comfortable change, and strangely, his outmoded WC350N had been replaced by a state-of-the-art WC400S. Well, that's not so shabby. How considerate. Clearly there is an afterlife, and it's definitely an improvement on life."

"Surely that'd be an afterdeath rather than an afterlife," a familiar, if muffled, voice responded to his thoughts.

Rock nudged his talking cushion, prompting Neville's next muffled quip: "Right, so I'm stuck between Rock and a hard place!"

After a moment's silence for a dead joke and a look of recognition between cushionee and cushioner, the WC400S sprang to life. No network logo. Straight to the message. "That's unusual," Rock said.

"No more unusual than being paged in a derelict shearing shed after having been koshed by a baseball bat wrapped in wool," Neville added.

This time a key difference between the 350 and 400 was apparent. The message came verbally with a soothing, interactive screen saver.

"The time is 4:00 p.m. You have been unconscious for 1.35 hours. During this time your world has changed significantly. We apologize for the interruption to your life and hope that you will remain a loyal, satisfied customer for many years to come." A brief tone was emitted, and Neville's and Rock's "digi-cuffs" sprang open.

The two cautiously exchanged looks and made for the door. A warm sun greeted them, and Rock noticed that he was somewhere that he had never been before. It was a flat plain spotted with gum trees and drenched in the remnants of the floodwater.

Neville, on the other hand, had a pretty good idea where they were. "Town's about twenty miles that way," he said, pointing. "That tractor will get us there."

Rock didn't even know for sure that tractors still existed, let alone how to drive one.

"They do, and I do," was Neville's reply.

Why was it that Rock still faced a challenge coping with Neville's telepathy? He'd twigged to it some time ago and it would have definitely given Neville and advantage in Customer Care.

"Because you still don't, really, believe in it," Neville replied, adding to Rock's exasperation.

*   *   *

As the tractor gurgled its way through the floodwaters, the coincidence that the aged farm vehicle had a full tank of fuel didn't escape their notice, but they both decided not to broach the subject at this time.

As they approached Lower Mullumdabba, two black hovercopters with vaguely familiar semicircular logos, circled in a frenzy overhead like flies over a fresh-baked apple pie—enticed by the smell but deterred by the heat of the crust. The hovercopters persistently charted their progress. Upon arrival on dry land, on the town's perimeter, one 'copter landed.

Rock's boss, Charlie Jones, leaped from the door and shook him by the hand.

"Great work, lad. Great work. No. More than great. Bold work, lad. That videotape was magnificent. Made syndication. Well done."

Neville had thought of Rock as a lot of things before, but never a lad. Yet Rock seemed to be basking in the praise and adoration.

"How did you find her? How did you get it?"

"It wasn't easy." As inane as it sounded, that was the only response that Rock could think of that would camouflage his utter confusion.

And Charlie bought it. "Great stuff! Skill, lad. Skill. Who'd have thought it—exclusive footage of Julia Folgate, only days after her husband's death, and talking with . . . My God, how did you do it?"

Charlie Jones had the ability to fire a succession of questions without taking a breath and without ever providing the opportunity for the questionee to answer.

Picking up from where their minds had stalled was "My God, how did you do it? Reginald Hargreaves, CEO of C&C Ent . . . you take the cake, lad."

There it was again—*lad.*

Rock's mind raced. He'd never thought of himself as a lad. Still, he was certain that it was some form of archaic compliment, and compliments of any type had recently been in short supply.

Still, Julia Folgate, Reginald Hargreaves . . . When? Where? How?

The redhead, the wake, the hovercopters, *C*s and *C*s on the pockets of Pure Newe wool suits. The dreams of rolling *C*s.

It all began to fall into place in the lad's mind.

Where better to meet than at a wake in a town isolated by floodwaters? Actually, Rock could think of hundreds of places that he'd prefer to meet to discuss a merger or a takeover; he prided himself on his active imagination. Then again, maybe that was why he would never be likely to need to meet to discuss a merger or a takeover confidentially.

That was the "when" and the "where"; the "how" might take a little more time.

Rock continued to consider the "how" as Neville raised Rock's hands above his head. "Our hero." *Ouch!*

Both men briefly reeled, jolted by a mild electric shock from Rock's wrist. The lens on the WC400S swiveled, taking in its . . . taking in its . . . environment?

Rock's mind went, *What the* . . . Neville's mouth went, "Later—catch you tonight."

"Absolutely," Rock replied. "Dinner at seven?"

"You bet." And Neville was on his way.

Your Action Plan

Quick Tips

1. ....

2. ....

3. ....

Summary

1. ....

2. ....

3. ....

Actions

1. ....

2. ....

3. ....

CHAPTER 16

DINNER AT EIGHT

N eville sat alone sipping cold alphabet soup. *C*s floated past as he contemplated the day's events.

It was an hour past seven when the joyous revelry of a hero broke the silent slurp of soup on a solo spoon.

With a slap on the back and a "How's it goin', old Nevie?" Rock was by his side.

"So, what ya reckon's happenin'?" Rock glanced toward the doorway where two largish men stood briefly and then disappeared. The *C*s on the men's jackets were so obvious. How had Neville missed them before?

Rock raised himself unsteadily from his seat. "Come on, party time, old Nevie."

Then Rock realized—why talk? So he quickly thought, *Something's wrong. Everywhere I go, there's large men in woolen suits, and people keep patting me on the back and handing me drinks.*

Neville twigged. "Party time, me old matey. Absolutely." He slapped Rock hard on the back.

Now was that really necessary? Rock thought.

"Absolutely, me old matey. Absolutely" Neville replied with another slap.

They stood and walked toward the door.

Rock's next action was prompted by Neville's words—"You don't look well, mate."

Rock grabbed his mouth, gagged, and then ran for the washroom. Neville followed.

As Neville entered, he was greeted by a gray-haired man. "Fred, Customers at the door—buy us time." Neville instructed.

As Neville and Rock discussed the past hours, Fred greeted the two largish men. He smiled. "Nice coats. Love the insignia." The compliment-sensitive embroidery immediately responded by doubling in size. "Pure Newe Wool too."

"Aah, yes." Embellished large man number 1.

"Great material. Durable. Warm in winter, cool in summer. Or so the young lambs say." Added large man number 2.

The *Cs*, sulking at the attention given to the material, contract to half their original size.

"Absolutely. And the cut and colour. Perfect. Must make you proud to wear it. You must be doing well." Coaxed Fred.

"Yes. Yes, actually I am." Large man number 1's chest swelled—literally!

"So am I!" interjected large man number 2.

"Good for you. So what brings you to these parts? I bet the two of you are pretty much the top of your profession. Not often we get people like you here." The Customers looked around. "No, not the washroom—Lower Mullumdabba. We don't often get prosperous professionals like you in these parts."

Slowly, gently, Fred won the men over. Soon the Customers were explaining how nice it was to be out in the country since they usually worked in the city. They were peripherally involved in virtual shopping, which didn't let them get away much. It was nice just to hovercopter out and see the real world occasionally.

After some time, Rock walked past them, pretending to wipe his mouth after pretending to rinse it clean. Neville slapped him on the back with a "Don't mix your drinks next time, matey!"

Fred bid the Customers farewell. "Thanks for chatting. Have a great time here, gentlemen," he said and then disappeared.

Retreating to Neville's house, Rock was astounded at how long Fred was able to occupy the men. "How did he do it?"

"Great Customer Service," Neville said. "Fred was one of our best at helping Customers feel important by showing interest in them."

*   *   *

How did Fred so effectively serve the largish men's needs and so distract them from Rock and Neville?

- The "Givens":
- active listening
- common courtesy
- open friendly and close positively
- smiling always—before, during, and after

- always thanking your Customers and thanking yourself for a job well done
- positive language, such as:
"Absolutely."
"Certainly."
"Excellent."
"Perfect."
"Yes, definitely."

Your Action Plan

Quick Tips

1.

2.

3.

Summary

1.

2.

3.

Actions

1.

2.

3.

CHAPTER 17

WHERE TO FROM HERE?

Rock became briefly distracted, perusing the photographs on Neville's mantelpiece as Neville prepared coffee. Photos of The Store, The New Store, and the new The Store ran sequentially across the mantel.

Calling to Neville, he asked, "The man is Redman, yes?"

"Absolutely!" Neville confirmed.

"The redhead, Julia?"

"Perfect!" Again Neville validated Rock.

Rock's eyes stopped at a photo of a loading dock. "Hey, those two thugs. They work for C&C now. Defectors?"

"Not really."

"But they're the ones . . ." A confused Rock briefly hesitated.

"Baseball bat . . . ?"

Neville added to Rock's confusion by responding, "Yes. Julia does get a bit theatrical at times."

Rock stopped, puzzled, and rubbed the lump on his head. Yes, it was definitely there. He had been hit—and hard.

Neville entered the room, noticing Rock's pain and confusion. "Would you like me to ask Dr. Fingle to look at it?"

"Ah, no. So where are you?"

"He's there." A mellow female voice oozed the information. "Next to me."

Neville returned with four espressos, to be greeted by a warm, very friendly kiss from Julia. Rock's mind immediately jumped to the plot of a bad police drama from the previous century—love triangle, Neville kills Redman and makes it look like suicide, marries his lover, and lays claim to The Store empire. Case solved!

"Now, how to release the story? Should it be a serialized article? Could it make syndication?

"Maybe a subscription e-zine or a C&C Ent e-Cast with interactive questions and dramatizations!" Rock said.

"Slow down; even my mind is challenged keeping up with this. K-I-S-S," Neville reminded him.

"Absolutely. Keep It Simple, Stupid."

Neville nudged the idea a little further with, "Try—Klever Indents Sensational Surgery."

"Klever with a *K*?" Rock's mind stopped in its tracks. "What?"

"Don't blame me. I didn't name it."

"They're a very discreet cosmetic surgery team headed by Dr. Fingle," Julia clarified.

The silence was broken by a quiet tap on the door, followed by the entrance of Fred Williams.

Julia called him Billy and greeted him with a hug.

"Hang on." Rock bought time as he tried to get his head around things. "That's Billy?"

"Billy to my friends, yes. Christened Fredrick Williams. My name was also my father's name. I hated 'Jr.,' so I got Billy for Williams."

"Bottom line?" Rock blurted out.

"Absolutely. I knew the 'lad' would get there," added Neville in an unusually fatherly tone. "Here's what happened."

"He's a journalist," scolded Billy.

"He's a friend," Neville reminded him.

"A journalist."

"A friend."

"Journalist!"

"Friend!"

The information loop between Neville and Billy could have continued into the night; Julia took it upon herself, however, to breach the gap and explain how things had happened. She pieced together

- their shared dream to reinvent "Customer Service" as "Customer Care" because it had become interchangeable with "Satisfied Customers" and treating Customers like sheep;
- Dr. Fingle's relationship with the Folgate family;
- the body in the mountain retreat—Redman's, with the help of Dr. Fingle and some zombie juice made from Billy's bees (Dr. Fingle coincidentally was, of course, the local coroner.);
- easy access to plastic tubs and sheep dip in Mullamdabba;
- Dave teaching Red to "read between the lines";
- the money that was needed to really start again and to achieve true excellence in Customer Care—through C&C E-nt's purchase of the old store;

- Redman's belief that it was essential to create a sense of ownership for both Incoming and Internal Customers; and
- of course, Redman's name (He loved Mexico, Mexicans, and the Spanish language, so what better than . . .).

At this Rock piped up. "Okay, this bit I have. Redman Folgate became Neville Roman."

"More Rojo-man than Roman," added Neville. "Rojo, as in Spanish for *red*, and Neville, as in *nuevo* equals *new*."

At that, Julia said, "The New Redman. And he says I'm theatrical."

"What's the thing with sheep, though?" Rock asked.

"Redman loved sheep, especially his black-faced Merinos bred from Mexican Tzotzils and Merinos—"

Interrupting Julia, Neville added, "Sheep are very special. C&C E-nt liked to treat Customers as sheep. That'd be fine if they treated them like my sheep, but they don't; they treat them like . . . like . . ."

"Like, really badly," Billy supplied.

Your Action Plan

Quick Tips

1. ....

2. ....

3. ....

Summary

1. ....

2. ....

3. ....

Actions

1. ....

2. ....

3. ....

CHAPTER 18

THE ORIGINAL AND BEST

The streets of Lower Mullumdabba had at last dried. A small podium stood in front of The Store. Over the building hung a larger banner that read:

Welcome to the Virtual Headquarters of The Store
The Original & Best
Brought to you by C&C E-nt

The band played, and somber, disbelieving locals mixed with enthusiastic "rent-a-crowd" teams as C&C E-nt officials spoke of a wondrous future.

Lower Mullumdabba would be put on the map as the center of the virtual headquarters for a virtual empire, a shopping experience beyond most people's dreams—all the service associated with The Store combined with the convenience of never actually needing to go anywhere or talk to, meet, or in any other way interact with any real person.

No longer would The Store be accessible to mere millions through its front doors; now billions of people would enter its portal on their PDAs, EFAs, wrist communicators, and for those in the very remote areas that progress had yet to reach, their trusted palmtops and PCs.

There would be no shop fronts, of course, and no real people. This would keep C&C E-nt's Customers "satisfied" by keeping prices down.

C&C E-nt guaranteed that all the service that people had grown to expect from The Store would be there at one's fingertips. No need to meet and talk with anyone. The "-xperience" would be a comprehensive virtual shopping excursion, including fully programmed avatars that would "guarantee you service with every click."

Each avatar had a name, like John or Billy or Anne or even Neville, just like the staff from The Store, and they were all programmed with exactly the same phrase patterns that had been developed in The Store—the same positive, reinforcing, friendly terms—repeated over and over again with no emotion, no sincerity, and no genuine care!

On the podium, Julia graciously thanked Reginald Hargreaves for his very generous check and handed him the keys. With Redman out of the way and the anachronistic institution that was the physical presence of The Store equally well removed,

Hargreaves cut the Pure Newe wool ribbon with his golden scissors and decreed The Store "open for business" . . . and closed forever. As these strange words floated among the crowd, video screens linked directly to The Store's e-page showed live video footage from around the world, as every The Store was imploded simultaneously to illustrate C&C E-nt's vision of the future—a future that applied all of Redman's service principles electronically.

With a crash, the back of the Mullumdabba The Store collapsed.

They would, of course, keep the facade of the Mullumdabba store to use for poster advertising, e-mmercials, press junkets, and special events. It had, after all, been classified by the Heritage Authority. The facade would hide a new multimegawatt satellite transmitter dish to expand C&C E-nt's rural coverage—a boon to the area, of course.

Julia watched in amazement and then quietly departed the podium, with ever so slight a sparkle in her eye. All local eyes turned and followed her.

Neville, Billy, and Rock joined her as she made her way through the crowd to a small, shrouded vacant lot across the street. A long cord hung from the shroud.

As Julia grasped the cord, silence filled the street. One tug, and the covers sequentially fell, first revealing a cocoon from which a butterfly banner emerged:

Welcome to Your Store—
Home of Customer Care

A second banner was unveiled, and it read:

Your Store—
where we treat every Customer as we want to be
treated when we're a Customer.

Then a third:

> *Your Store—*
> *where everyone is a Customer—not merely a shopper.*

And finally, accompanied by a butterfly logo:

> *Welcome to the death of Customer Service*
> *and*
> *the Birth of Customer Care.*

Your Action Plan

Quick Tips

1. ....

2. ....

3. ....

Summary

1. ....

2. ....

3. ....

Actions

1. ....

2. ....

3. ....

CHAPTER 19

WHO KILLED CUSTOMER SERVICE?

As a small lamb sat quietly in the corner of an enormous New York bookshop, surrounded by enthusiastic converts to Customer Care, Rock Hardstuff signed copies of his acclaimed book: *Who Killed Customer Service? The Story of Your Store, My Store, the Store.*

An eager, freckled boy fired questions at him: "So, who did kill Customer Service?"

Rock replied in a practiced, almost tutored fashion. "The answer is not who, it's what: time, progress, changing expectations, and the evolution of ideas. Ultimately our expectation to be treated as real humans. Being treated with Service Excellence killed Customer Service. I guess you could say that Customer Care killed Customer Service."

An attractive redhead walked to the signing desk. Rock's eyes started at her legs and worked their way up. *Nice*, he thought. A graying gentleman by her side added, "Yes, and she's mine."

Rock smiled as he looked up.

The gentleman added, "I'd like to talk with you about Customer Recovery. Dinner at seven?"

"Absolutely perfect!"